JOYCE

ALAN HINES

Order this book online at www.trafford.com
or email orders@trafford.com

Most Trafford titles are also available at major online book retailers.

Print information available on the last page.

ISBN: 978-1-4907-8802-9 (sc)
ISBN: 978-1-4907-8803-6 (hc)
ISBN: 978-1-4-907-8810-4 (e)

Library of Congress Control Number: 2018938770

Trafford rev. 03/22/2018

Trafford PUBLISHING® www.trafford.com
North America & international
toll-free: 1 888 232 4444 (USA & Canada)
fax: 812 355 4082

BOOKS OF POETRY ALREADY PUBLISHED BY ALAN HINES,

1. Reflections of Love
2. Thug Poetry Volume 1
3. The Words I Spoke

URBAN NOVEL ALREADY PUBLISHED BY ALAN HINES,

1. Book Writer
2. Queen of Queens

UPCOMING BOOKS OF POETRY BY ALAN HINES,

1. Reflections of Love (Volume 2, and 3)
2. This is Love (Volume 1, 2, and 3)
3. Founded Love (Volume 1,2, and 3)
4. True Love (Volume 1,2, and 3)
5. Love (Endless Volumes)
6. Tormented Tears (Volume 1,2, and 3)
7. A Inner Soul That Cried (Volume 1,2, and 3)
8. Visionary (Endless Volumes)
9. In My Eyes To See (Volume 1,2, and 3)
10. A Seed That Grew (Volume 1,2, and, 3)
11. The Words I Spoke (Volume 2, and 3)
12. Scriptures (Volume 1,2, and 3)
13. Revelations (volume 1,2, and 3)
14. Destiny (Volume 1,2, and 3)
15. Trials and Tribulations (Volume 1,2, and 3)
16. IMMORTALITY (Volume 1,2, and 3)
17. My Low Spoken Words (Volume 1,2, and 3)
18. Beauty Within (Volume 1,2, and 3)
19. Red Ink of Blood (Volume 1,2, and 3)
20. Destiny of Light (Jean Hines) (Volume 1,2, and 3)
21. Deep Within (Volume 1, 2, and 3)
22. Literature (Volume 1, 2, and 3)
23. Silent Mind (Volume 1,2, and 3)
24. Amor (Volume 1,2, and 3)
25. Joyce (Volume 1,2, and 3)
26. Lovely Joyce (Volume 1,2, and 3)
27. Pink Lady (Volume 1,2, and 3)

28. Mockingbird Lady (Volume 1,2, and 3)
29. Godly tendicies (Volume 1,2, and 3)
30. Enchanting Arrays (Volume 1,2, and 3)
31. Harmony (Volume 1,2, and 3)
32. Realism (Volume 1,2, and 3)
33. Manifested Deep Thoughts (Volume 1,2, and 3)
34. Poectic Lines of Scrimage (Volume 1,2, and 3)
35. Garden of Love (Volume 1,2, and 3)
36. Reflection In The Mirror. (Volume 1,2, and 3)

UPCOMING NON-FICTION BOOKS BY ALAN HINES,

1. Time Versus Life
2. Timeless Jewels
3. The Essence of Time
4. Memoirs of My Life
5. In my Eyes To See
6. A Prisoner's Black History

UPCOMING URBAN NOVELS BY ALAN HINES,

1. Black Kings
2. Playerlistic
3. The Police
4. Scandalous
5. The West Side Rapist
6. Shattered Dreams
7. She Wrote Murder
8. Black Fonz
9. A Slow Form of Suicide
10. No Motherfucking Love
11. War Stories
12. Storm
13. Ghetto Heros
14. Boss Pimps
15. Adolescents
16. In The Hearts of Men
17. Story Teller
18. Kidnapping
19. Mob Ties

PRAYER

Heavenly Father I thank you for being wonderful, for being marvelous, for loving me regardless. Always being there resolving problems. Thank you for blessing me to live to see another day. Never leading me astray and always being there to whip my tears away.

After rain shining your sunlight for better brighter days. Unconditional love that shall never fade or perish away. Although mom is gone I pray that she will reach and enter Heavens gates upon judgement day. In Jesus name I pray.....Amen.

Acknowledgements

First and foremost I always choose God first; I thank him for everything. I thank my grandmother Jean Hines, and my mother Joyce Hines without them through God I wouldn't even exist; I'm grateful for all the love they showed me throughout life; I wish they could've lived forever may the rest in everlasting, eternal peace. I thank my family, and friends that has been loving, and supportive to me. I even thank those people who have showed me no love, no support they helped me to become a better me more sulf sufficient and disciplined.I thank those that even took out time to read any one of my other books. I hope all those that decide to read this book enjoy, and God Bless You.

JOYCE

JOYCE

1. CONGRATULATIONS MOM

Congratulations mom u got your wings.
Don't worry about the kids and grandkids we good within reality
as it seems.
Gooo.....Mom gooo.....spread your wings go go up to Heaven,
meet the king of kings.
Spread your wings get away from all these no good Earthly things.
You finally got eternal peace reality not a dream.
No more worrying no more pains.
I love you mom but it's time to move on to bigger and better things.
Go mom spread your wings glorify and sing.
You finally became one of God's angels mom you get your wings.
I see you in Heaven mom you look so pure skin so clean wow God
gave you
your youth back he turned you back nineteen.
Love you mom my queen of queens.

2. I Love You More

Mom I love you more and more although now you rest in eternal peace.
Don't worry in Heaven your mom, brothers, and my grandfather and family
and friends once again you shall meet. Mockingbird lady let your soul fly,
fly away to finally be at peace. For the first time in person Jesus Christ and his
father you shall meet. I must admit life without just aint gonna be sweet. A genuine unconditional love always came from you to me.
Finally in Heaven finally at peace.
Mockingbird lady fly away and be free.

3. ATLEAST

Atleast you was always there.
Atleast I could count on you in times
of despair when no one else gave a care;
you was there when no love from others appeared.
Always had a place to call home, you gave keys
to the city, a major factor, a mayor.

4. YOUR ARE MISSED

Your are missed throughout the seconds each minute of the hours.
Lady of timely power.
Soul shall stand tall like a tower.
Memories shall never fade pleasant visions on
my mind shall remain devour.
Remember when you was a teenage nectar providing flower.
You're loved and missed throughout timely sessions each second
minute days of our lives with the 24 hours.

5. CHOICE

Freedom of speech.
Freedom of choice.
Love hearing your name through each
and every voice.....Joyce.....

6. Nightly Visions

Nightly I vision you wearing a crown a queen.
On your back sits enormous fluffy white wings.
Lovely lady of dreams.

7. A Love Like No Other

A love like no other.
I was hers she was mines she was my mother.
There's no greater love than that from a mother.

8. LOVELY MOTHER

As my lovely mother lay down to sleep I
pray the Lord her soul to keep.
Even if I should die before I wake I pray the Lord
my soul to take.

9. HONOR

In the Bible it says honor thou mother
and father.
Mom although your gone I love even more regardless.
To your seeds your were marvelous.
Sometimes you used profanity to express problems
but you was always there through it all
and was always marvelous.

10. FULLNESS

And then came the stars the sunlight and the fullness of the moon.
Mom hopefully judgement day will appear so youll be going home
to
Heaven soon.

11. REJOICE

Rejoice for this lovely lady named Joyce.
After a bottle her opinion she'd voice;
made noise.
Lovely lady Joyce.
At Christmas time you made it rain
with the gifts and toys.
Extended love throughout the projects of
girls and boys.

12. CONTINIOUSLY FLOWING

Your first born love you to death shall
forever mourn.
Your family seeds still growing.
Legendary legacy of blossoming memories life through
us continously flowing.

13. JUST LIKE MAGIC

Magic.
Love that was satisfying.
Gratifying.
No denying,
Love that's everlasting.

14. THANK YOU

Thanks you for the life that was giving.
Love of life as a wonderful feeling.
A reflection of you through the creator as one
of your children.
Rest easy at peace in the eternal paradise
as a Heavenly citizen.

15. LOVE UNTO YOU

Love unto you.
Love and respect that's forever due unto you.
Memories that shall never fade anew.
Visions of you when you were young in your youth.
Days holding my hand walking me to grammer school.
Sweet melodies of a flute.
Lady sing to me the blues.
Wishing I could've been more of a better son to you.
A seed that grew.
My lady of love, love unto.

16. MY LOVELY MOTHER

Red roses on a pink and white casket of unforgettable love.
Only for you I'd shed blood.
To reach you I'd swim through infested waters of floods.
My lovely mother, my love.
As a kid at times I complain about the things we didn't have,
when I should've been grateful of what it was,
motherly love.

17. BEGOTTEN SON

Mom this is what it's become.
Your touch of gold, your magic wand.
Your begotten son.
A life built off the triumphs over struggles
of great aspects to come.
Without you I wouldn't exist,
or even have anything under the crescent moon slash sun.
On top I shall make myself a winner, I already won.
It's me mom, proud to be your begotten son.

18. FOREVER EXIST

In my mind, body, soul you forever exist.
My childhood tooth fairy, my every year female Kris Kringle
that possessed the wish list.
My queen of queens my womenly prince.
You definitely will forever be missed forever exist.
Thanks for being a mother to the twins, even through timely events.
Thanks for being a mother and a best friend with most gracious
bliss.
Thanks for everything, through me you forever exist.

19. Dear Lovely Mother

Lovely mother.
Never be another.
I love you like no other.
I promise to look over my younger sisters and brothers.
Shedded tears alone under covers.
Still working hard on manuscripts taking life further.
I can't believe your six feet under by dirt smoother.
A love like no other my lovely mother.

20. WHITE BIRDS

Lovely white birds fly from palms
of hands, fly, go far away.
Live to see another day.
In the skies with no limits forever stay.
Never perish away, even when it becomes the
darkness after the light of day.

Lovely birds don't let the other birds lead you astray,
fly, fly, far away go your seperate ways.
Lovely white birds fly far away.
Stay in the sky forever at your utmost high.
Spread your wings high as the sky.
Chirp lovely white birds, chirp in the morning as the sunrise,
light up the skies, chirp and forever fly,
to forever rise.
Lovely white birds fly.

21. Enchanting Arrays

At night I watch the sky, it's enchanting array.
I love you in a special way.
Memories and visions shall never perish,
shall never fade.
A lovely parade.
Definitely a product of what God made.
It's flowers of bouquet.
Happy holidays.
Sweet dreams as above the clouds you lay.

22. ALWAYS TRUE

Let your love shine through.
Love was always true.
Skies that turned blue.
My heart is always near you.

23. PAINT A PICTURE

Paint a picture mom for I can see it, up in the sky high.
Paint the sky.
Paint a vivid picture of your surroundings
in paradise with wings to fly.
Paint a picture of the love you receive once you reached
paradise, and open your eyes.
Paint a picture of when I was a kid,
you and I together by your side.

24. GIVING REASONS

In any giving reason it was nothing but love throughout
the season.
Continiously breeding.
No matter the space or time within
disagreements, the love kept breathing.
Hunger feeding.
Always had place to call home
with the changing of seasons.
A heart of gold and enjoy pleasing.
Never switched up throughout seasonal conversations
of seasons.
Loved for any giving reason.

25. REMEMBRANCE

I remember you vividly of yesterdays that past.
From when I was a baby, adoloscent, formulated to a man.
You was always there.
A round of applause raising of right hands.
The best friend I ever had.
Peoples person smiles to make each one laugh.
Never leave no one in the cold they always could
come live with you to rest their head.
Remembrance, visions shall never fade or past.
Lovely woman fly away to meet the Angels upstairs.

26. NUMBER ONE

My number one, favorite girl.
Red roses, and pink swirls.
Precious lady to me you mean the world.

27. FAR AWAY

Far away, love shall stay.
I pray for you everyday.
Eternal life above the clouds you rest, to lay.
Birth right of me you made.
Love you and miss you more each day,
although you gone far away.

28. LOVE BEYOND COMPARE

Love beyond comparison.
Love beyond despair.
Love that was always here
love that's always there.

29. A GIFT

A gift that keeps on giving.
A life that keeps on living.
We are all God's children.
Spread your wings of love like
a eagle in the skies with no limits.

30. LOVE MOM

Love Mom.
Days of light kingdom shall come.
You shall be the Goddess of the rising sun.
Love, struck, amazed, and stun.
Proud begotten son.
Lord open up the gates here she come.

31. NOURISHMENT FED

The nourishment of love fed.
Stay ahead.
Love you rather breathing or dead.
Miss you mom inner tears to forever shed.
Thanks for blessing me with life instead,
the great advice, breaking bread each
slice you had.
Lay down mom, relax your body,
peace within head.
Rest in eternal paradise luxurious bed.

32. LOVE LIKE NO OTHER

A love like no other.
The bearing of siblings, sisters and brothers.
Keep taking me higher, taking me futher.
The unveiling of curtains, behind door number ones cover.
The blindfold of a child I complained about unfinancially stable
burden being smoothered.
As a adolescence and beyond life futher I seen that you'd give
anything to me, my sisters, and my brothers,
there was no greater love, love like no other.

33. INSTEAD

Living and breathing instead.
Happiness no tears to shed.
One of the only true friends I ever had.
Richer or poor, sickness and health, living
breathing instead.

34. LOVE INDEED

Indeed love was always granted acheived.
Never cease to amaze, never cease to breathe.
Food for thought, food for the mind body, and soul to feed.
Mother nature, motherly love indeed.

35. SPREADED WINGS

Spread your wings sing.
Do away with all Earthly things.
Sail freely down streams.
Walk through the tunnel of eternal life that gleams.
Thank God for each and everything.
The day shall come when you meet your maker the king of kings.

36. TO

To a different place within time, shine.
To a fresh start an all new beginning, the paradise of love, no worries no sinning.
To a great life with no ending, but to the contrary a brand new beginning.

37. BLOSSOM TO GROW

Planted of a seed to blossom to grow.
Oh how we love and miss you so.
From lack of rain, damaged soul still had the ability to grow.
Taught me many of things I know;
not to be judgemental accept people for the way they rocked they
way they flow.
Take small bits and pieces making them to enormous loads.
Family matters as planted seeds to blossom to grow.

38. YEARLY SESSIONS

Yearly sessions.
Blessings.
Learn lessions.
Confessions.
In peace resting.

39. TO SEE YOU AGAIN

Wonder will I ever see you again.
Will I see you smile, to hug me,
to talk to me again.
My mother, my friend.
Wonder when my Earthly body become deceased
and my corpse is stuffed in a coffin and put six feet
under within, will I then see you again.

This day and age I do Godly things amongst
the brothers and sisters of Christ on God's land.
Righteous hearts of men.
Once upon a time I lived a life of sin representing
for those affiliated under the golden star of the fin;
therefore I wonder if within Heaven God will allow me in;
but I pray daily that you and I will be forgiving for all
our sins and be allowed above the clouds together once again
Heaven within, to see you again.

40. FOREST OF RAIN

Forest of rain.
Love in abundance for you I'll make it rain.
From you in which I came.
A realist lived your life with no shame.
Memories ease the pain.
Forest of love forest of rain.

41. SHE, HER, I, WE

She, her, I, we.
Growth as her planted seed.
Nourishment to feed.
Love indeed.

She, her, I, we.
Spiritually, her love shall forever be.

42. SHARE

Shared your life,
shared your world.
The creator of life
three boys four girls.
My diamond my pearl.
Center of attraction,
ruler of demonsional worlds.
Thanks for it all thanks for sharing your
world.

43. I CAN'T LET GO

I can't let go, I can't never move on.
Stuck in a time frame, a terrible war zone;
where the souls of falling soilders roam.
Like Dorothy following this yellow brick road,
I just wanna go home.
In loving memory your name lives on.
Non-judgemental thou whom has not sinned cast the first stone.
Although you gone your love and legacy continously roams,
forever lives on.

44. LOVELY STAR

A star to guide my way.
Loving in a special way.
Blessed the day.
For you each day I pray,
that, that a star will guide
your spiritual spirit my way,
and forever stay covered by the blood of
God's son, in which him we trust,
to sleep in peace to lay.
Staring at the skies for your star to guide,
guide the way.

45. BLESS THE CHILDREN

God bless the children.
From soilders to civilians.
Those resided in mansions to those
section 8 low income living.
Bless those that's poor to those worth millions.
To the Haitians to the Africans, to
Americans, to those all the way in New Zealand.

God bless the child, God bless the children.

46. PAINT

She painted this beautiful ribbon in the sky.
I see it's held/shown high in the sky.
Setting in the East as the sunrise.
I still remember when you had the Jerry curl,
shoe laces you taught me to tie.
Never left my side.
Never ending unconditional love ties.

I see the ribbon in the sky a sign
of the times, letting me know you'll
always be by my side.
You watch over me in stormy weather of life
as I drive, as demons and sickning villings coincide.
When I feel pain I see the rain drops as tears you cry.

47. MADE ME

You made me feel so wonderful.
Beautiful.
Masterful.
Magical.
You made me feel power, powerful.
You made me feel so wonderful.

48. CREMATED ASHES

Consumptions, turned into nightmares of you laying in a casket.
True colors of two faces was unveiled from maskes.
Lucifer controls the masses;
Free choice of decisonal mind sets.
No attendance no love no support in arrangements
in eternal closes of eyes.
The falsehood of love, rumors, and lies.
Live forever through your seeds hearts,
minds and visual sight of eyes.
Pour out a little liquor and allow
your cremated ashes to blow away in the skies.

49. LOVE TO GROW

I love you so.
Love to grow.
Memories can't let go.
Caped crusader, a hero.
A blossoming of flowers,
trees, and babies to grow.
I love you so.

50. GREATEST

I proudly hold my head to the sky.
Never questioning the creator why you had to perish
to fly.
Knowing someday we all must leave this Earthly flesh
when it's time,
rather or not we have been baptize.
Angel in eyes.
My great lady never changing tides.
Family ties.
Dignified stride.
My lady of light the greatest of all times.

51. BREED

Allow the seed to breathe.
To breed.
Teach and lead.
Knowledge to feed.
No-abortion give birth to achieve.
Indeed.
Proceed.
Seeds to breathe.
Adults lovely childrens to breed.

52. THROUGH ME.

Live through me.
Set your soul to fly away, be free.
Glow, shine throughout eternity.
Forever be at peace.

53. CANDLES

Candles burning, missing, and yearning.
Lessons taught, experiencing was the best
teacher of learning.
On June the 9th there should be candles
burning held by latter day saints right before sermon.
Hearts burning.
Candles lite as a reflection of your light shined in the darkness
of nights before the sunlight in the morning.
We love you out here making you proud performing.
Candles stay lite stay burning.

54. ETERNITY

For your seeds succeed to breathe.
Efforts to acheive.
Promises to do good deeds.
Your love and remembrance shall last throughout eternity.

55. THEN

And then she gave birth to four ladies and three
best men.
A mother and a friend.
Close together like twins.
Be allowed in Heaven, father forgive us all
for our sins.

56. LIKENESS

In the likeness of her.
A precious lady you were.
Cut from a different cloth like animals of fur.
You were someone that I'd admire, adore more.
Enjoy you journey your tour.
Each day away I love you more.

57. MOTHER MAY

It seems like yesterday.
Little kids to play.
Tears I cried you'd whip them away.
I shall never go astray.
For you lovely poetry I'll convey.
Good things about you I'll always say.
Mother may I, can I, mother may, peacefully lay.

58. MEMORIES

Memories forever lives on.
Love stands strong.
Kids all grown.
Your house was like no other place to call home.
Memories forever lives on.

59. A Superstar

A superstar.
A all-star.
A movie star.
A shining star.
A star that I love from near and far.

60. COME BACK

Never perish away.
Walk my way, talk my way;
I'm interested to listen to anything you have to say.
I want you to meet my wife even before my wedding day.
Let's go to church together on sundays.
Wake me up for school on mondays, I promise to get good grades.
Visions of the truth shall never fade.
Come back, come back to life within upcoming days,
we need you here to stay.

61. All Times

Times when I had nobody,
you was everybody.
My birth right, my holidays,
my parties.
You'll never leave me stranded,
never not even probably.
All times my lovely lady, my dolly.

62. AWAKE

Upon your awake from your peaceful sleep;
Heavenly allow her soul to be free.
Life she gave me.
The best part of me, she forever be.
Loving memories.

63. WISHING

Wishing she could've lived forever or we could've
died together.
Loving you whenever.
My lady super woman my lady hero
of the same rare feather.
Never forget the love that didn't change in seasonal
weathers.
Provided shelter always for family and friends that
had no where else to live to rest whenever.
Didn't judge those that use substances or had
different sexual preference not even the sexual predators.
But I need her by my side when I become a bestseller.
I wish she could meet my wife when I decide to get
married who she may be whoever. I wanted my kids future kids
to love you better.
In place on my own still grinding for the cheddar.
I need her no one will love me better.
Rest in peace rest in paradise rest in Heaven forever.
Thanks for the life you gave wish You could've lived forever or
I wish we could've died together.

64. FREED ME

Freed my soul.
Watered me with knowledge as a seed
and watched me grow.
I love her, I love her so.

65. PROUD

I promise that here on Earth I'll make
you proud.
I'll please you amongst the crowds.
Glorify your name out loud, a reflection of
you as your begotten son, proud.
Your love child.

66. STAR

I'm wishing on star to follow where you are.
I'm wishing a dream, Heavenly as reality as it seems.
I'm wishing on star to follow where you are, to let you know I
love the same rather near or far.

67. SLUMBERS OF DREAMS

I see you in visions, in slumbers of dreams.
A nightingale that once upon a time walked the
Earth and would sing.
Your son the prince of you the queen.
Sleep tight, be at peace, and have sweet dreams.

68. SORROWS

Sorrows, knowing it will be better
days tomorrow.
Rain drops, afterwards the sun, the rainbows with
pot of Golds to model.
For thee alone I worship,
and only him I shall follow.
Hopefully we will meet again
as angels once the Lord
comes back to get the souls
of his followers.

69. CHILDHOOD MEMORIES

Childhood memories filled with
all the wonderful things you did for me.
Christmas trees Mrs. Claus without a chimney.
Provided all my needs.
Birthdays were always made happy.
One love for the family.
Memories of you being astonding.

70. LIKENESS OF GOD

Created in the likeness of God.
Beautiful like the shining sun, the moon, the stars;
First spaceship to Mars.
Beginning of a new life thus far.
Freedom for the innocent ones locked behind bars.
As a newborn being born with no defects or disablity scars.
In the likeness of you, through him Father God.

71. MY ANGEL OF PARADISE

I see you within times of young and older, fullest of life.
Gave me life.
My angel of paradise.
I see you got wings that was used to take flight.
I seen you go, go up above the skies out of sight, to meet
the Heavenly Father and his son Christ.
No faded memories, forever part of my life.
Memories of delight.
Memories haunts me day, and night.
Memories of you always being there even
when my life was cruel and unusual punishment,
although I wasn't right, I had you my angel of paradise.
A shining light.
Without you it wouldn't have been easy surviving life.....
My angel of paradise.

72. HAPPY MOTHER'S DAY, EVERYDAY

After the rain comes sunny days.
Every single day wishing you a Happy Mothers Day.
Happy Valentines Day.
Lovely one shine my way.
For you to reach Heaven upon judgement day I pray.
Happy Mother's Day everyday.

73. GONE

I can't believe you gone, I can't get you outta my mind outta my life.
Rebirth live forever, have a second life.
Deserved to live thousands of years after Christ.
Love you more each day for the rest of my pending life.
I pray that you shall have eternal life in the garden of
Eden in paradise.

74. Coming

The coming of days.
The coming, approached beautiful smile.
Be with me for the long hall, all the while.
Beautiful lady, beautiful Godly child.

75. Missed and Loved

Know that you are missed and loved.
My truest of truest love.
For me I know you'd shed blood.
Spreaded wealth, spreaded love.
Missed and loved.

76. Fly Away

Fly by day.
Fly by night.
Gave good love.
Gave good life.
Fly so high days and nights.
Great unconditional love reaching new heights.
Shining of love even in the darkest nights.
Fly, fly high days within turned into nights.

77. SHAME

It's strange how things became.
Those that she loved glorified thou names.
Upon life itself for them she would've did anything.
Upon the funeral came what a shame you
embarrassed her name.
Didn't put up any finance for the funeral to be arranged.
Didn't even come to show last respect to her as
Heaven gained.
In God we should always trust,
not human beings.
They say don't trust strangers but sometimes
strangers will treat you better than those
family and friends in your own lane.

It's strange how things turned out.
It's strange how things became.

78. ANEW

Anew.
Something sweet as ripe fruit.
Peaceful and tranquil as low tone
of jazz,
melodies of flute.
Love that'll never undo.
Love that had always been true.
Anew.

79. FREE LOVE

I think of she as the sun set in the East.
I think of she a festival, a daily fest.
Beauty crushes the beast.
Complete.
Special way to be.
Happiness to free.
Casting away bad spells that was to be.
Swin freely through seas, free.

I think of she freely being free.

80. VOICE

How I wish I could hear your voice.
Lovely lady come to life, make some noise.
Take me back to a kid as you flourished me
with gifts under the tree, female Kris Kringle of toys.
Let me hear something, say something, make some noise.
Let's rejoice.
my lady, my fair lady Joyce.

81. LOVELY TIMES

A gold mine.
A life line.
A life without racist hate crimes.
Holy and divine.
Happy Sweetest Day,
Happy New Year,
Merry Christmas,
and Happy Valentines.
Loving all the time.
A peace treaty signed.
A rhythm, a rhyme.
Loving at it's best kind.
Love all the time.

82. EXCITED

Excited.
Delighted.
Brighted.
Sighted.
Upscaled, uprighted.
Nourished appetite, tighted.
Excited, delighted.

83. FAMILY TIES

Family ties, souls arise.
Hope, and opportunity keeps love alive.
All winners of the prize.
Another new life babies born came alive.
New borns being baptize.
Blooming of youth to adults to produce
more lives.
Family keep growing, family ties.
Through her many are blessed to be living
continuos growing of lives.....
Family Ties.

84. BEGINNING

A new beginning.
The land of angels of no sinning.
Once enemies becomes friends.
Brothers and sisters women, and men.
No more pains, worries or struggles again, eternal no end.
Where deceased family members, and friends shall
meet again.
It didn't end it just begin.

85. RED ROSES, FLOWERS OF KISSES.

Red Roses, flowers of kisses.
Blood stains of potraits of pictures.
Hot flashes of hearing your conversated words
as still in existence.
Of you constant visions.
Repitition of scenes of you laying in the hospital
bed relentless.
For you I write/recite the deepest poetry as if you were here
listening.
Forever red Roses, flowers of kisses.

86. Shared

Shared everything.
Lady of giving life.
My lady of dreams.
My queen.
My queen of all queens.

87. LOVING GRACE

A loving grace.
A warming heart, a shelter, a pleasant place.
A forever smile upon face.
A remembrance, never forsake, or deface.
God makes no mistake.
The realness of love nothing fake.
Did whatever it takes.
At the end of each day I pray that
to the finish line you'll make.
Loving, grace.

88. SHE'S IN PEACE

Atleast she's in peace.
Made it up stairs to relax to be at ease.
Crushing Satan dragon of the beast.
Spread your feathers angelic elite,
in peace.

89. ABOVE SKIES

Midnight stars in the sky.
Mom, I hate that you had to perish away
from vitilaty of existing ties.
Drowning tears to cry.
Forever spiritually by my side.
Lovely angel fly away to a better place
above the skies.

90. TIME FLIES

Time flies.
We all are living to die.
Caskets of last goodbyes.
Through me lives forever never shall die.

91. Enchanting

Enchanting array.
Orchids of pink mini bouquet.
Thou shall not go astray.
The loveliest of lovely days.

92. LOVE

Love beyond compare.
Love as she really cared.
Love unbreakable, even from others forbidden, rare.
Love that was always there.

93. ESSENCE

Time is of the essence.
Time spent is precious.
You're truly a blessing.
Time is of the essence.

94. SENSATIONALLY

Sensational, sensationally.
The greatest reflection of me.
Spreaded your feathers, wings,
fly away don't look back or you
shall be cast to stone to be;
just fly away, and be free.

95. APRICOT

Fruitful multiplying Apricot.
Everlasting love feathers cut from
the same cloth.
Beautiful creature of God.
Bottom to the top.
Monumental statue, stone, rocked.
Multiplied affections never cease
to amaze, never stop.
No secrets told greatness of plots.
Multiplied gave your all fruitful
freely apricot.

96. ANCHOR

Lake shores.
The world is mines,
the world is yours.
I adore, amor.
Can I get an anchor.

97. DIVINE MAJESTY

Divine majesty.
Loving her loving she.
For I am her she is me.
What a wonderful lady she
is she be.
Your highness, your majesty.

98. BE AWARE

To be aware is to be alive.
To have everlasting life after ashes
to ashes dust to dust blow away through
summer breeze to skies.
Holy waters to be baptized.
Awarness to be alive have a heart to
forgive through eternal everlasting
blood line ties.
To be aware is to be alive.

99. SEPERATIONS

Seperations distinguishing differences
of genuine to the fake.
Seperations of being sanctified
away from the Devils burning rakes.
Celebrations celebrating
reaching the pearly gates.

100. MAINTAINING

She taught me to watch for constant dangers.
Love all but don't trust even your own
friends nor strangers.
Knowing that life is filled with
overcoming obstacles some wont be painless.
Reframing.
Earning, gaining.
Substaing, and maintaining.

PREVIEW FOR UPCOMING BOOKS

TRUE LOVE

POETRY

1. Free Love

The same air we breathe.
Together happiness acheived.
A special lady, a special part of me.
Love for us to see.
I love her she loved me whole-heartidely.
Love that was free.

2. LOVELY, AND COURAGIOUS.

Sensational,
motivational,
all the time not occasions.

Couragious.
Love contigious.
Abnormal, love in abudance outragious.
A performer of stages.
A memory of love that could never be faded.

3. CHERISHING CRUSH

For her I had a cherishing crush,
A fondness I loved so much.
When apart I couldn't wait to get together to kiss, hug,
hold hands the gentle touch.
There was no one as her, or just I we was together as one us.
An enchanting overwhelming crush.
Us forever together is a must.
I adore you so much my sweet lady,
my cherishing crush.

4. THROWN

In the comfort of our love zone.
A special designated place we called home.
Would never leave you alone.
Study ways to make you feel like a queen of a thrown.
For you wrote poetry, sent you text messages of love,
each time you were away from home.
Knew and appreciated the woman you've came to be,
oh how you've grown.
An all star of comfort, of love, of a pleasurable tone,
a love I could call my own, a love for my queen of the thrown.

5. PARTIPATED

Participated.
Congratualted.
Under rated, before her time out dated.
Finally made it.
Struggled and strived to be successful
through hard work dedication and patience.
Participated.

6. SIMPLY MEANT

Simply marvelous.
Like a special event.
Time well spent.
Heavenly, Heaven sent.
Fresh like mints.
A natural perfume scent.
Simply adorable, you and I were meant.

7. ARRAY OF SUMMER

The enchanting array of summer.
Someday I'd make you my spouse, and a mother.
To me you are an excellent lover.
A friend that always encourages me to go futher.
Your mom and dad made a lovely daughter.
Your dreams I promise to be more supportive.
Guidance and order.
The enchanting array of summer, summer's daughter.

8. HURRY

Some say you shouldn't rush it,
but her love came in a hurry.
She seemed to be stress free, never worried;
she put everything in God's hands that was her true story.
She didn't date to much, didn't have any kids wasn't interested in
watching
Maury.
She was genuine she let love come in a hurry.
Kept her mind and body clean wasn't poisioned or dirty.
Stayed in library of books to be an impending professor
she was worthy.
She was there in my time of need lovely lady, lovely flurry.
Her love came fast in a hurry.

9. COMPLETE ME

Complete me.
Freed me.
Would travel across the globe to see me.
Wanted always be near me.
Together is where she wanted us to always be.
My lady of liberty.
My lady Mermaid of the sea.
The one completed, please never leave.

10. POWERED LIVES

Empowered lives.
Kept the youthfulness, and desire of love, and hope alive.
An inspirational pride.
Within her chaos, and confusion and been died.
Side by side, as loyalty and affection coincide.
Continued to step, and stride.
The excitement even stayed alive.
Touched the heart and mind of others by empowering lives.

11. REFRESHING DELIGHT

A refreshing delight.
An Earthly paradise.
A straight path, the ways of being right.
The love of life.
Sunny days that came even after the darkest nights.
Refreshing delights.

12. A Wonderful Feeling

Oh, what a wonderful feeling.
The love that was being giving, fufilling.
Home, always live, living.
Pleasure was all mines, a privilege.
Always able, and willing.
The loveliest love, my queen of hearts
of dealings.

Oh, what a wonderful feeling love that
was being received, and giving.

13. TREND SETTER

Enjoyed my poetry, and love letters.
A trend setter.
Second time around she always tried to make things better.
She'd provide shelter for the homeless so they wouldn't be stuck
out in the bad weather.
Cut from the same cloth, birds of a feather that flocked together.
Whatever I decided she was down for whatever.
She'd dream of freedom like the late great husband of Coretta.
She'd read my poetry out loud, but secretly read my love letters.
She told me to keep writing, and things would get better.
She was fashionable, a designer, people followed her trend,
trend setter.

14. I Wish

I wish....
I wish to spend, savour each moment together
as a bliss.
Luscious lips to kiss.
Swim through seas like schools of fish.

I wish you could be an adult that made Santa Clause
gift list.

A queen for a king, a princess for a prince.

I wish we could live a life alone without a plot
or twist in a world as we're the only two that exist.

I wish....

15. THAT GIRL

That girl has my heart plus mind.
I love more each time.
Symbolic signs.
A queen of hearts, divine.
The best of times.
Her and I as one combined.
That girl is so fine proud to have her mines.

16. LIFE'S ENTIRETY

Her life in it's entirety, shall gave me it's all.
She'd stand me back up after a fall, letting me know
you must walk but only after you crawl.
Loved me throughout my exterior flaws.
She'd go against the Judicial system if I decided to break the court
systems
laws.
She gave my love, and devoted her life with no pause.
She gave me everything in it's entirety,
she gave me her all.

17. SPECIAL KIND

Never misunderstood.
Stimulates, stocks of woods.
Created atmospheres, all good.
Wishing our love to forever remain, wish it would.
Special kind, special kind of love as it took a stand,
stood.

18. STANDS

Stand for something or fall for anything.

Stand on your own two feet, legally an
adult at the age of eighteen,

Stand back up even after you fall, as it seems,
women and men, kings and queens.

19. WHEN LOVE CAME

When love came.
An intoduction, love at first sight
a mutual feeling of being the same.
Kept me sane, able to maintain.
A stimulator, a peace maker, through brains.
I definitely could gain.
Fortunate and fame.
A love that was righteous, no loop holes
or anything.
My everything.
My princess, my queen.....
She even wanted to have my last name.
When love came.

20. BELIEVE ACHIEVE

You gotta believe that greatness you
can and will achieve.
Success is a must indeed.
Spouses should, must be appreciated,
and please.
Fathers provide, feed.
Unlock all the positively, with positive keys.
Believe, achieve.

VISIONARY

1. Motivational Keys

The motivation I need to succeed,
to provide, feed.
Do good deeds.
Forever grateful of being freed.
Giving it my all at a full speed.
A given jewel, a planted seed.
Letting all the good and bad motivate me to succeed;
motivational keys

2. EFFORTS

Timeless efforts of not studying lessons,
brought forth stressing,
not realizing I should be counting blessings,
not stressing, but utilizing taught lessons.
No sins for confessions.
Bearing gifts, presents.
Accomplishing goals, by putting forth best efforts.
Being grateful for life, as living is precious.

3. INVISIBLE, VISIBLE

Invisible, but should've been visible, 3-d dimensional,
of intentions, hidden agenda of extended hand shakes
that's giving to you.
A secret meaning of text messages to you.

Couldn't see the invisible, obviously intentions,
suspiciously be-friend you.
Sometime the invisible becomes visible to,
other times invisible remains near sided to you.
You thought that they was a friend to you,
invisible to the scandals that women and men premeditate
and eventually do.

Invisible, and visible To

4. DIFFERENTIAL

Clause,
Purpose,
Meaning,
Definition,
Defined as,
Surpassed,
Outlast,
Outcast,
Upper and lower class,
Happiness turned sad,
Good and bad,
Mom and dad,
Frowns and laughs,
Different laws passed,
Different generations as time passes.

5. WISDOM

Abolish all non sense giving.
Learn lessons from inmates in prison, that made bad decisions.
Be more understanding and listen;
accept constructive criticism.
Be grateful to be one of God's children, still living.
Enjoy wonderful feelings.
Stand tall as ceilings.
And control all dealings.
Properly raise children.
And let wisdom do all healing.

6. LIFE TO LIVE

Too much life to live,
so I'm living better than it already is.
Head to the sky conquering fears.
I'm a grown man now so I whip away tears.
Not saying what I want, waiting on someone to give
going out to get it in the days of our lives,
throughout years.
I got my own life to live.
The man up above gave me this life to live so let me live.
But yet and still it is what it is in this life I live.

7. TOMORROW

Tomorrow will bring more better, brighter, beautiful things.
Living out our dreams.
Daily birds chirp and sing.
All hail to the new born king, and all the wonderful things another
day tomorrow
brings.

8. I MUST

I must continue breathing,
signing contractual agreements.
Twins and N'dia I must continue feeding.
Success seeking.
Leading.
Goodness breeding.
Allowing life to have it's meaning.

I must continue breathing, feeding,
knowledge seeking, to the word being obedient.
Proud to be one of God's creatures, and letting his
legacy live on through features.....

I must continue breathing.

9. GOOD ADVICE

At times you got to let go,
move on with life.
Realizing that you only live once not twice.
But always think twice.
Do what's right, make wise decisions come to life.
Do the good things you like.
Listen, follow, take heed to good advice.
When it's all said and done seek that place
formally known as paradise.

10. REMAIN

Remaining sane.
Keeping it simple and plain.
Living your own life doing your own things.
Chaos reframe.
Currency through success was gained.
Pleasant bells that rang.
The love, life, and loyalty was everything,
that remained.

11. GOD IS GREAT

God is good, God is great.
Thanks to him I was given life to live today, and yesterday.
Bombs, and semi automatic weapons they continue to create, but
thanks to him I'm safe.
Rent is paid I have a pleasant place to stay.
For me a job and a publishing house he created.
Destine for greatness through his fate,
knowing that his everlasting love could never parish or wash away.
And I love and appreciate him more each day.
I definitley worship a God that for my sins allowed his only son's
life to
be taking away.
Oh yes I pray each day to an awesome God whom is good and
great.....
God is good, God is great.

12. Heed

Sometimes but not all you must turn the other cheek.
In time the inheritance of the earth shall go to the meek.
You gotta swallow pride, take heed, lead to succeed.
Hard work brings forth achieve.
Knowledge is power that feed.
Be careful of the food you eat, the toxic air you breathe.
Let life be a lesson, learned, taking heed.

13. FRUITFUL

Be fruitful and multiply.
Wishing you'd live forever never die.
Keep your head to the sky;
as forever worship the creator above the sky.
Be grateful for the simple things that come by.
Just look at those in third worlds,
from hunger and lack of doctoring they die.
Love all, and trust none of any kind.
Keep working hard knowing some day you'll be fruitful,
and multiply, as a light shall shine.

14. Be

Let things be what they be.
Be observant, to see what you see, reality.
Allow inner spirits to be free from captivity.
Stand tall like the statue of liberty.
When it's said and done be who you be;
without trying to fit in to false proximity.
Be, be free.

15. FOCUS MORE

Focus more on spiritual guidance,
scripitual abiding.
Letting good intentions come out of hiding.
Top of the line presidential residing.
Displaying kindness.
Positive moves, smooth sailing, cruise control ridings.
Making wise decisions within deciding.

16. SUBSIDIARY RIGHTS

Non-fiction and fiction being brought to life.
Creatively write.
Red, blue, and black ink of sight.
Typing words all through the nights.
Peaceful uplifting stories, and others of violent fights.
Making it happen, not wondering what might.
Fans wondering when the next story will be orderable through sites.
Quaterly royalty checks being flown like kites.
Advancements of substantial likes.
Day and nights write.....
Controlling subsidiary rights.

17. ABSTRACT

Abstract.
Snap back.
Statements of facts, is only an opinion not a fact.
Missing pieces of the map.
Those that left and wont come back.
Getting lives on track.
Trying to get the real thing back from being abstract.

18. LIFE GOES ON

Stregthen my bones,
for those that's dead and gone.
I love and miss you, but life goes on, I must carry on.
Using the good qualities in you that was past along.
Often I see your kids and they're all grown.
Wish you was still here to live long.
Your legacy carries on.
But I must carry on.
Life goes on.

19. REPLENISHED BEGINNING

Replenished beginning,
baptized, born again Christian.
Life without sinning, forgiving,
blessed to still be living.
With anew beginning, happy ending.....
Replenished beginning.

20. MOMENTARILY

A momentary sign of relief.
Filing briefs, praying to the skies that appeals, and/or Habeous
Corpus shall set 'em free.
Remembering those that's deceased, forever resting in peace.
Food for third world's to eat.
A place to be free.
A love of life to be.
Amazement never cease.
A momentary sign of relief.

21. GOD GAVE

God gave me life,
courage, and sight.
Days I pray to him in the morning and nights.
God is my protector days within and even in the darkest night.
God gives me a vision, sight, a grip of light,
a path so I could be prosperous through his will,
and might.
God gave me life, courage, wisdom, understanding and sight.
He gave me life.....

22. As It Is In Heaven

Let it be done on Earth as it is in Heaven.
Give us this day as a daily bread.
Lets thank God in which we worship and thank him first instead.
Thank him for guiding us through to the straight path, and not leading us astray
as being misled.
Giving us the fulfillment of life to live breathing living, clothing, sheltered, sheild,
and fed.....
Let it be done on Earth as it is in Heaven, as food for thought,
as a daily nutrition of bread.

23. IT IS

It is what it is.
God is the only one I shall fear.
Constant funerals of tears.
Living each day as a Merry Christmas, and a Happy New Year.
Knowing people and things, come and go, and disappear.
I live life as a realist sincere.
Each day I thank God I'm still living, still here

24. LETTING GO

Sometimes you gotta let go.
It's no room, space, outta time to grow,
that poor performance considered as a relationship
you gotta let go, it's never going to amount,
never gonna grow.
People, places, and things you may love so,
but those that are no good, let go.
Give your ownself the love and respect to grow.

25. BE GRATEFUL

Be grateful to have a place to live.
To be a father or mother to kids.
Graduated to the new millennium;
another year still living here.

Be grateful, and sincere.

Be grateful that it is what it is,
still living still here.

REFLECTION OF LOVE

VOLUME 2

1. THE CITY OF ABUNDANT LIFE

She was from the city of Abundant Life.
Prayed to God through Jesus christ.
Sanctified is the way she chose to live life.
A virgin like Mary, Joseph's wife.
She made others take flight.
High off scriptures, and life.
Fun-loving, and nice.
For each one offering she gave twice.
Didn't care of others downfalls, or sick sinful delights;
she'd still preach to them about Christ.
She said once she die, she'd wanted to be buried
in the city of Abundant Life.

2. THANKS LORD

Thank you Lord for allowing me to wake up today to breathe.
To continue on with life, to proceed.

Thank you Lord for giving me a golden heart that loves doing good deeds.

Thank you Lord for giving me a paper and pen to write poetry as a way
of being free.

Thank you Lord for the clothes on my back, the food that I eat;
thank you Lord for simply blessing me to be me.

3. EVER

It was said the love we had would remain rather we're breathing or dead.

The only true love I ever had.

My happy days was converted over from the once tears I shed.

She'd convey to me her feelings out loud and sometimes with a pen and pad.

Since the day we met no regrets, I'm glad.

She say she's pregnant, so now they start calling me dad.

A love that brought forth riches from rags.

The only true love I ever had.

4. LOVE BOAST

Not to brag or boast.
You the one I love the most.
An everyday champagne toast.
My ex-lovers are like ghost.
Keep you close;
a love I never want to let go.
You understand my style, my grind,
hustle and flow;
the love of poetry in which I wont let go.
It's so many reasons why I love you so.

Not to brag or boast but I truly
love you so.

5. TREE OF LIFE

Her love came like the tree of life.
Genuine natured, that of another time,
maybe I met her before in my former life.
The love of my life.
Her love was right I only wanted it once for the
rest of my life;
didn't want to break up and do it twice.
She faithfully served God,
and prayed to him each day as a latter day saint,
through Jesus Christ.

Her tree of life was right.
She kept her body, as a temple of righteous delight.
In life she wanted to do things that was right.
She loved me day and night.

In her back yard she had the apple tree of
red apples that was ripe.
It was nothing like the tree in which Eve, Lucifer, and Adam
brought sin to life.
It was the tree of knowledge, wisdom,
understanding, and love of life.....

The tree of life.

6. FINESSE

In the most magnificent, beautiful, wonderfulest way she finesse.
Her love was better than the rest.
Her heart and mind she gave made me feel blessed.
Made me feel the firmness as an exercised chest.
Her love she gave it all and nothing less.
She'd never settle for less.
A way to be free from stress,
only her and I no contest, finesse.
I confess that I love the way she finesse,
better then the rest.

7. MY ANGELS

They're my angels,
my Godly childs.
I love them all the time not only once in while.
The four together drives me wild.
Blessings as my kids, Godly childs.
I pray throughout life you'll over come tribulations and trials.
Allow God to be your guide all the while.
I'll be there through God later and now.
My angels, my Godly childs.

8. ANY GIVING SEASON

Any giving season her aim for pleasing was because
of I, me breathing.
Together never leaving.
From chaos fleeing.

Any giving seasons she stimulates my brain by teasing knowledge
feeding,
increasing speeding.

Any giving seasons she loved me for each and every reasons.

9. BABY N'DIA

I know you're only a baby,
and babies cry.
Sweetheart don't cry whip the tears from your weeping eyes.
Know that I love you, live for you,
for you I'd die.
That's one of the main reasons I write books of poetry,
erotica, urban so you can live down here on earth as it is in the sky.
Have a large piece of the pie.
A reflection of my truest love, and please don't shed a tear even
when I die.
A love for one of mines.
Baby N'dia you and I.

10. CELEBRATE, AND SING

Celebrate and sing.
Enjoy life in it's entirety, everything.
Appreciate life even the smallest simplest things.
Be your on light that gleam.
For knowledge fiend.
Be greatful for blessings,
celebrate and sing.

11. A LOVE

A love that was so much.
To hot for rumors, and the fakes to touch.
Much more, a plus.
Wonderful wonder woman that I met at work through an
appealing crush.
Oh how I love to kiss, and touch.
We on the same page, share the same dreams to fulfill
as a must.
I talked she'd listen, she'd talk I'd listen to her, together us.
No argurments or fuss.
Soulmates together as one, us.

12. SATISFIED WITH LOVE

She satisfied me with love.
Always peaceful no matches of grudge.
A love that flood.
Could even turn out clean things from stains of mud.
An angel from the Heavens above.
Her voice was like music to my ears because;
because she'd satisfy me with her love.

13. RIBBON

A ribbon that made me feel like I could fly.
Conquer any, and everything while living, alive.
One of my many reasons to live,
and I'm just not ready to die.
A ribbon in the sky.
A ribbon of love mutual together as a tie.
The realness I just couldn't deny.
A ribbon, a ribbon the Godly sky.

14. COINCIDENCE

It was more than a mere coincidence.
A love that was meant.
Time together well spent.
Growth of a woman, growth of a man.
Together we stand as lovers, and friends.
Hope we will grow old together until our life ends.
A blessed love that was no coincidence.
In the end came wedding vows, and pregnancy of twins.

15. Someone I Wanted To Know

Someone I wanted to get to know.
Feel, touch, and see how you flow.
Together, grow.
Continue to go.
I wanted to love her so.
Us together until we grow old.
From a distance I'd watch her,
and my eyes wouldn't let go.
I'd study her motions and distant ways,
and wanted I know.
Know in her head what goes on.
What knowledge she withold;
future plans, and goals.
I wanted to know if she was even interested in me
to get to know.

Someone I wanted to get to know,
and maybe share a love like no other I've
ever known or had before.

16. Remember Like This

Remember like this loyalty of a bliss.
Luscious lips to kiss.
Even when I'm not around remember like this.
The giving gift of love like St. Nick.
A princess, and be the prince.
Remember me and represent.
Together the precious time spent.
Whisper shoftly in my ear as love was meant.
Remember all the good times we shared,
the pleasurable moments spent.
Was there at my worst and my best.
Remember when for you I was much more than a lover or friend,
remember like this.

17. I HOPE

I hope that we can make it.
A love that was genuine no faking.
Rebuking of Satan.
I hope we make it happily congratulated.
A love that will be forbidden, forsaking.
Permanent stationed.
Always appreciated.
Glad, no regrets, didn't mistake it.
I want us to forever be together,
I hope we make it.

18. AND THEN

And then she converted her life over to Christianity,
never again in life would she sin.

And then she spreaded her love, and kindness to
the women, children, and men.

And then she treated me like an aspiration of love
that forever with held, suspend.

And then she'd chant softly to me day, and night
that she'd always love me with no end.

And then she became my first wife, gave birth
to my first son, the little brother of my twins.

And then the saga continues on, a love with no end.

And then.

19. SUNSHINE WITHIN

You made sunshine come in.
Afraid to lose you I know another you I'll never find again.
She said before me she never laid up with another man.
She had long black curly hair, creamy white skin adored by many men,
but she was even more beautiful within.
When I was only twenty something years old, she, her made ma feel young again.
Even at 12:01 a.m. her light of sunshine would shine in.
When my spirits was down she'd lift me up,
when I needed a helping hand, she'd always be there a true friend.
She had a special ability to glow in any and every room she came in.
Quite often she'd sit around reading nothing but religious material in the Den.
I loved the way she shined to contend, my sushine within.

20. SWEET LIKE CANDY

Sweet like candy.
Fine and dandy.
Polite and friendly.
Loving by the tons, plenty.
Never met alot of others like her,
not many.....
Sweet like candy.

21. EYE APPEALING

Eye appealing.
Wonderful feelings, high as sealings.
Successful dealings.
Strived for a better living.
Life was for the giving.
Played Ms.Claus during Christmas for the children.
Put forth efforts to do great things through genuine feelings,
eye appealing.

22. TRUTH, REAL

She is the truth, and so real.
I love the way she makes me feel.
My lady hero, my wonderful woman of steel.
Provided massages, and medicine to cure my painful sickness of ill.
Would vividly express to me daily on how she feels.
Loving that was for real, and I definitely could feel.
On top of that she made her own money went half on the bills.
She never wanted to argue or debate she just wanted love to be the deal,
and love it to feel.
The truth so real.

23. Valued

Appreciated,
valued,
adored,
love I found you.
A dream that had came true.
A lovely lady a woman, a new.
My queen to be appreciate, and valued.

24. GARDEN OF LOVE

Garden of love.
An angel from up above.
Warm hearted love that peacefully flowed,
a natural continious flood.
Fresh fruit of produce,
wholesome vegetable to share even with strangers
as if they were family of the same blood.
So filled with joy, peace, and love.
A dynamic duel of solutions to add more there of.
A back yard, a place to call home, a garden of sensational love.

25. LADY FIVE

Lady five kept the destiny of everlasting love alive.
Four she continiously opened up beautiful doors.
Three she allowed me to be free.
Two she let it do what it do.
One she earned it my love was won.